EXPLORE
TOKYO

by Douglas J. Fehlen

STORY LIBRARY

www.12StoryLibrary.com

12-Story Library is an imprint of Bookstaves.

Photographs ©: Puiipouiz/Shutterstock.com, cover, 1; gowithstock/Shutterstock.com, 4; apiguide/Shutterstock.com, 5; Marzolino/Shutterstock.com, 6; National Land Image Information (Color Aerial Photographs), Ministry of Land, Infrastructure, Transport and Tourism, 7; Benny Marty/Shutterstock.com, 8; PJ_Photography/Shutterstock.com, 9; Sean Pavone/Shutterstock.com, 10-12; Scirocco340/Shutterstock.com, 13; cowardlion/Shutterstock.com, 13; SandraSWC/Shutterstock.com, 14; Joshua Davenport/Shutterstock.com, 14; Richie Chan/Shutterstock.com, 15; cowardlion/Shutterstock.com, 16; TK Kurikawa/Shutterstock.com, 17; Kobby Dagan/Shutterstock.com, 17; Bit Boy/CC2.0, 18; IQRemix/CC2.0, 18; J. Henning Buchholz/Shutterstock.com, 19; 7maru/Shutterstock.com, 20; Guillermo Olaizola/Shutterstock.com, 21; Phubes Juwattana/Shutterstock.com, 22; Marcelo_Krelling/Shutterstock.com, 22; f11photo/Shutterstock.com, 23; Page Light Studios/Shutterstock.com, 24; Korkusung/Shutterstock.com, 25; Kobby Dagan/Shutterstock.com, 26; MOROZ NATALIYA/Shutterstock.com, 27; Korkusung/Shutterstock.com, 28; seeyah panwan/Shutterstock.com, 29; f11photo/Shutterstock.com, 30

ISBN
9781632357311 (hardcover)
9781632358400 (paperback)
9781645820185 (ebook)

Library of Congress Control Number: 2019938660

Printed in the United States of America
September 2019

About the Cover

Tokyo Tower, the second-tallest structure in Japan.

Access free, up-to-date content on this topic plus a full digital version of this book. Scan the QR code on page 31 or use your school's login at 12StoryLibrary.com.

Table of Contents

1

Tokyo Has a Mild Climate and Dramatic Geography

The Rainbow Bridge over Tokyo Bay.

Tokyo is in the center of the Japanese archipelago. It is located at the top of Tokyo Bay on the Pacific coast of Japan. The city is the nation's capital. Also called Tokyo Metropolis, it extends west from Tokyo Bay to inland mountains. Its area covers 846 square miles (2,191 sq km).

Greater Tokyo includes three surrounding prefectures. Low plains lie to the north. To the west are mountains. Mount Fuji is the most famous. South of the city, two groups of islands extend into the Pacific Ocean.

Tokyo has mild winters. High temperatures average between 50 and 56 degrees Fahrenheit (10 to 13°C). Summers are often hot and humid. Temps can top 95 degrees Fahrenheit (35°C). Spring and fall bring a lot of rain. Yearly precipitation totals just over 60 inches (152 cm).

Mount Fuji with the landmark Chureito Pagoda in the foreground.

May to October is typhoon season. The Japanese word for hurricane is *taifu*. A typhoon is a tropical hurricane. Typhoons bring heavy rains and strong winds. They can cause landslides and floods. Transportation is interrupted. Sometimes homes are destroyed and lives are lost. Tokyo experiences two or three typhoons a year, mostly in September and October.

386
Area in square miles (1,000 sq km) of Tokyo Bay

- The bay has an average depth of 53 feet (16 m).
- Natural and human-made islands rise above its waters.
- Some islands are made partly from the garbage of Tokyo residents.

MOUNT FUJI

Japan's largest mountain dominates Tokyo's western skyline. Mount Fuji is 67 miles (108 km) from the city. It rises 12,380 feet (3,776 m) above sea level. The mountain is also an active volcano. It last erupted in 1707. At that time, volcanic ash fell over Tokyo. Many experts worry about another eruption. Some say it could bury the capital under three feet (1 m) of ash.

From Fishing Village to a Nation's Capital

The history of Tokyo goes back centuries. What is now a megacity began as a small fishing village on Tokyo Bay. Its original name was Edo. Starting in the 1600s, it became a political and cultural center. But it was not yet the nation's capital. That was Kyoto, a city 300 miles (483 km) to the west. Japan's imperial family lived in Kyoto.

In 1868, the imperial family moved to Edo. By then, Edo was Japan's largest city. The name was changed to Tokyo, which means "eastern capital." The city became the new capital of Japan. Rapid modernization followed.

Buildings were made with better materials. Communication systems improved. Railways made travel easier. In 1889, the Constitution of the Empire of Japan was created. It established the country's modern political system.

In the early twentieth century, many Japanese people moved to cities. Tokyo was a popular destination. A powerful earthquake struck in 1923. Fires roared through the city. More than 140,000 people lost their lives. An estimated 300,000 homes were destroyed.

The small fishing village of Edo, with Mount Fuji in the background.

23,000
Years ago when the area was first settled

- The site started as a fishing village.
- A castle was completed there in the fifteenth century.
- By the 1720s, the city was home to more than a million people.

Aerial view of the inner grounds of Edo Castle, the location of the Imperial Palace today.

Japan's role in World War II has shaped Tokyo's modern history. The nation joined Germany and Italy against the Allied powers. The city was bombed more than 100 times. The Allies won the war in 1945. Since that global conflict, Japan has sought international peace.

TIMELINE

3000 BCE: A village called Edo is established on Tokyo Bay.

1200 CE: Walls are built to protect the area.

1457: Edo Castle is completed.

1657–1698: Several large fires destroy much of Edo.

1707: Ash falls over the city after Mount Fuji erupts.

1868: The city's name is changed from Edo to Tokyo.

1923: The Great Kanto Earthquake destroys almost half of the city.

1927: Tokyo's first subway line opens.

1940: Japan joins Germany and Italy against the Allied powers.

1945: WWII ends when Japan surrenders.

1964: Tokyo hosts the Olympic Games.

1993: The Rainbow Bridge opens.

2013: Tokyo is chosen to host the 2020 Olympic and Paralympic Games.

Tokyo Is the World's Largest Metro Area

More than 13 million people live in the city of Tokyo. The greater metropolitan area has 38 million residents. This is a quarter of all Japanese citizens. Greater Tokyo is the biggest metro area in the world. It is also among the highest in population density.

Nearly all Tokyo residents are Japanese. Some come from the Philippines, Korea, and China. Two religions dominate. Shintoism is one. It is the religion of Japan's original inhabitants. Some people began practicing Buddhism in the sixth century. Many Japanese observe both faiths.

Tokyo's economy has been growing recently. But not everyone is doing well. There is a big gap in wages across neighborhoods. For example, people in Minato have an average annual income of 11.1 million yen ($98,000). That is three times as much as workers in the nearby areas of Kota and Ota.

View of the Tokyo Metropolis, the biggest metro area in the world.

Shinto priests wearing traditional attire.

People in Tokyo are known to be hard workers. Some have even died from working too hard. Enough people have passed away that there is a Japanese word to describe these deaths. It is *karoshi*. People worked long hours without getting enough sleep.

Tokyo has about the same number of women and men. But that does not mean equal access to opportunity.

Japan as a whole has a large gender gap in wage earnings. Women earn 73 percent of what men do for similar work.

THINK ABOUT IT

Men are paid more than women in Tokyo. Why do you think women receive lower wages than men? What can be done to make wages more equal?

846

Area in square miles (2,191 sq km) of the Tokyo Metropolis

- This is a small part—only 0.6 percent—of Japanese lands.
- The area is the country's most densely populated.
- Japanese travel to Tokyo for the best jobs.

4

Its Economy Is Bigger Than Many Nations

Many banks and insurance companies are located in Tokyo's financial district.

Tokyo has the world's largest metro economy. Its gross domestic product (GDP) is 179 trillion yen ($1.6 trillion USD). That is bigger than the entire economy of Canada. About one-third of Japan's national wealth comes from Tokyo.

Several industries help the city prosper. Tokyo has most of Japan's information technology (IT) and communications companies. It is the country's financial hub as well. Banks and insurance companies make major international deals here.

Tokyo is also a manufacturing center. Many companies create consumer goods. High-tech products are mostly created in the western part of the city. A hub of technology companies helps deliver smartphones, computers, and other devices to the public.

Many of Japan's largest businesses are located in Tokyo. Examples are Honda, Mitsubishi, and Hitachi.

THINK ABOUT IT

Why do you think Tokyo is an important economic center for Japan? What are some reasons why national and foreign companies would have offices in Japan's capital?

633,819

Number of businesses in Tokyo

- Half of Japan's largest companies are in Tokyo.
- More than 9 million people work in the city.
- Foreign companies place their Japan offices in Tokyo three-quarters of the time.

Many foreign companies are here as well. The city is also a center for international trade. Its port is the second largest in Japan for imports and exports.

Another industry critical to Tokyo is tourism. The city is among the world's top destinations. More than 12 million people visit each year. These tourists are important to the local economy. People in service industries especially rely on visitors.

Tokyo is one of the world's top destinations for tourists.

Tokyo Is Always Under Construction

Single-story buildings once spread throughout Tokyo. But natural disasters, wartime bombings, and a growing population changed that. Today most buildings in Tokyo last 30 to 60 years. Then they are torn down and replaced. The city has almost no empty land. Old buildings cost too much to update. The result is a modern metropolis, home to shiny skyscrapers and high-rise dwellings.

Towers ring Shibuya Crossing, the world's busiest pedestrian intersection. Thousands of people cross the streets every three minutes. Lit-up buildings are common in Tokyo. Projections light the night on the walls of Louis Vuitton, Christian Dior, and Prada.

Other buildings throughout Tokyo add to the skyline, day and night. Many stand dozens of stories high. Tokyo Skytree is the tallest at 2,080 feet (634 m). It is the highest broadcasting tower in the world. Other skyscrapers include Toranomon Hills and Midtown Tower. Both stand more than 800 feet (244 m) tall.

More pedestrians cross Shibuya Crossing than any other place in the world.

1914

Year when the Tokyo Station was completed

- The domed, red brick Tokyo Station is a popular attraction.
- It was badly damaged during World War II and nearly torn down.
- A major renovation that began in 2006 and ended in 2012 re-created the original station.

THE YANAKA DISTRICT

Much of Tokyo is very modern. But the Yanaka District is an exception. It has some of the most traditional Japanese architecture in the city. Narrow streets are lined with old wooden buildings. Shops, shrines, and temples are popular attractions. Unlike much of Tokyo, the Yanaka District survived Allied bombings in World War II. The area is popular among tourists looking to experience old Tokyo.

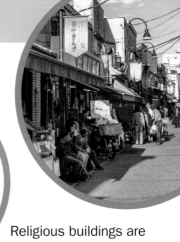

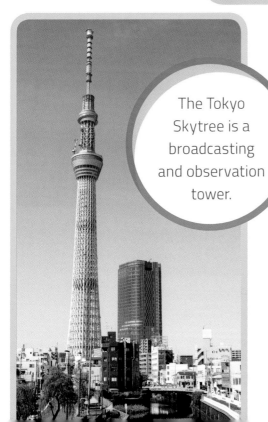

The Tokyo Skytree is a broadcasting and observation tower.

Religious buildings are other architectural highlights. St. Mary's Cathedral is laid out like a cross, with an exterior of stainless steel. Tokyo Camii is Japan's largest mosque, with much decoration. Tsukiji Hongwanji is a Buddhist temple resembling South Asian houses of worship.

Infrastructure Supports Travel and Business

Tokyo's railways are among the best in the world. Trains are known for being quick and on time. Bullet trains connect Tokyo to the rest of Japan. Some travel at speeds of more than 200 miles per hour (322 km/h).

There are Tokyo workers who commute by car. But traffic is often very bad. The government is now working to build a ring of three expressways. They

8 million
Number of daily passengers on Tokyo's subway system

- Shinjuku station averages more than 3.6 million riders a day.
- It is the busiest subway station in the world.
- Passengers leave the station from more than 200 different exits.

will extend outward from the city center. Officials hope this system of roadways will lower travel times.

Many people arrive in Tokyo by air. Flights land at Tokyo International Airport all day and night. Planes connect 48 Japanese cities and 32 international urban areas. Travelers can catch a flight to the city from 18 different countries and regions.

Another way people travel to Tokyo is by water. The city's harbor has terminals for cruise ships and water taxis. Boats travel to local islands as well as faraway countries.

Tap water is not safe to drink in many Asian cities. But Tokyo's water is cleaned. Local residents and tourists can drink it directly from the faucet. The water supply comes from nearby rivers.

Most people in Tokyo have access to the internet. So do all major companies. As a worldwide leader in new technologies, the city relies on fast connection speeds.

Tokyo's subway system is extremely punctual with trains arriving less than five minutes apart.

The Capital Is the Nation's Arts Center

Japan's arts capital is Tokyo. It has more museums and theaters than any other city in the country. Tokyo is also the national center for media and pop culture.

The National Art Center is known as one of Japan's most important art spaces. This museum does not have a permanent collection. Instead, contemporary works rotate in and out. The Mori Art Museum also has modern pieces. They are displayed more than 50 stories in the air. Cutting-edge artists' works are shown in the National Museum of Modern Art.

Other institutions focus on the past of the city and the country. The Tokyo National Museum is one. Statues, cookware, and clothing are some artifacts shown. The Edo Museum explores Tokyo's more recent history. Visitors learn how the city has developed over 400 years.

Tokyo is also a center for the performing arts. Theaters offer different styles of works. Kabuki is the most popular. Traditional

The National Art Center has one of the largest exhibition spaces for contemporary art in Japan.

The Kabuki-za is a famous theater where traditional Kabuki is performed.

dramas feature fancy costumes and decorative stages. Kabuki is performed at many city theaters. The National Theater of Japan is the best known.

World-class musical performances can be seen in Tokyo. The Japan Philharmonic Orchestra, Tokyo Philharmonic Orchestra, and Tokyo Symphony Orchestra hold concerts at area theaters.

WHEN THE SUN GOES DOWN

Tokyo is known for its vibrant nightlife. Museums, galleries, and other hotspots are often open late. People enjoy walking through the neon-lit streets of Shibuya and nearby neighborhoods. Diners feast on great food at sidewalk tables and rooftop restaurants. Tokyo's famous arcades also draw nighttime visitors. People pack city movie theaters as well.

117,000
Number of objects in the Tokyo National Museum's collection

- The Tokyo National Museum is the oldest museum in Japan.
- Its collections include 89 national treasures.
- A 120-year-old tulip tree grows in front of the museum.

People in Tokyo Love Sports

Baseball is by far the favorite sport in Tokyo. Two professional teams play in the city. The Yomiuri Giants club is beloved by millions. It sells out most games at Tokyo Dome. The Yakult Swallows have a large fan base as well. This club plays games at Meiji Jingu Stadium.

Crowds also support football (soccer). Two city teams play in the J1 League. FC Tokyo competes in the top division. Tokyo Verdy is a popular second division club. Both play in Tokyo Stadium. Japan's much-loved national football team competes in major tournaments like the World Cup.

Tokyo residents also enjoy individual sports. Track and field, swimming, and gymnastics are a few of the most popular. Boxing, judo,

SUMO WRESTLING

Sumo wrestling is Japan's national sport. It goes back to at least 712 CE. Wrestlers train from a young age to compete. They gain size with the help of a diet of protein and rice. Athletes also train mentally. Sumo competitions draw many Tokyo fans. Several Grand Tournaments are held in the city each year.

wrestling, and tennis are others. These activities are all official Olympic sports.

In 1964, Tokyo hosted the Summer Olympics. These were the first Games to be held in Asia. More than 5,000 athletes came from 93 nations. In September 2013, the International Olympic Committee (IOC) elected Tokyo to host the 2020 Olympics.

5
Number of times Tokyo has bid to host the Olympic Games

- The first time was for the 1940 Summer Games. Tokyo won, but the Games were cancelled because of World War II.
- Tokyo bid for the 1960 Summer Games but lost to Rome. It bid for 2016 but lost to Rio de Janeiro.
- For the 2020 Summer Games, Tokyo beat out Istanbul and Madrid.

Nature Surrounds the World's Biggest City

Millions of people visit Tokyo each year. It is not hard to understand why. The city has important cultural sites and architectural treasures. Natural wonders also draw visitors.

Mount Fuji is among the most famous mountains in the world. It rises over Tokyo's western skyline. Many people climb the mountain. The journey up and down can take a full day.

Nature also stars in other areas of Tokyo. Shinjuku Gyoen National Garden sits on 144 acres (58 hectares) west of the city center. It is most visited in spring, when cherry trees blossom. Forests lay outside Tokyo. Aokigahara is one. "The Sea of Trees" has popular hikes near Mount Fuji. The Meiji Shrine is in a forest that covers 170 acres (70 hectares). The Imperial Palace is in a large park with gardens and a moat. This is the primary residence

Cherry tree blossoms bring many visitors to Shinjuku Gyoen National Garden.

The Imperial Palace and gardens.

of the Japanese royal family, but the gardens are open to the public.

Several famous Tokyo sites are buildings. Some were built long ago. The Sensoji Temple is the city's oldest religious site. Raised in 628 CE, it draws 30 million visitors each year.

Other popular destinations are modern. Tokyo Tower is designed like the Eiffel Tower. One major difference is that it is painted bright colors. Built in 1958, the tower transmits radio and TV signals. Millions tour its observation decks and underground mall.

Many people also visit Tokyo's skyscrapers. Neighborhoods like Odaiba, Ginza, and Akihabara have buildings of steel and glass with shops and restaurants. They are often lit up at night.

10 million
Number of international visitors to Tokyo

- The total number of tourists is higher.
- Japanese people from other prefectures travel to the city in large numbers.
- Shrines and temples are popular spots, as are shops and parks.

People Travel to Tokyo to Eat and Shop

A teppanyaki chef prepares Kobe beef for diners.

Tokyo is ranked one of the best food cities in the world. This includes both restaurant food and street food. The city has 226 Michelin-starred restaurants. Paris has the next highest number, with 94.

Many Tokyo restaurants focus on popular Japanese dishes. Sushi is the best known. It is often a roll of cold rice with fresh raw fish and vegetables. Several courses of food make up a traditional Kaiseki meal. These are cooked in a variety of styles. And teppanyaki offers a dramatic dining experience. Diners can watch meals of meat, fish, and vegetables prepared right in front of them.

Tokyo also features international food. This includes quality European cuisine. French restaurants are especially common. Italian and Spanish eateries abound. Many establishments have chefs and kitchen staff who trained overseas.

3,600
Number of hotels in Tokyo

- The city's hotels have over 84,000 rooms.
- Many people visit Tokyo specifically to shop its department stores.
- The biggest is Isetan, which includes a building 10 stories tall.

TRADITIONAL MARKETS

Tokyo is known for its fancy department stores and boutiques. But some areas offer a more traditional experience. Asakusa is one. People at street stalls sell locally created arts and crafts. Tourists often stop here for souvenirs. Asakusa is just one of several traditional markets in Tokyo. Often these sites lay in the shadows of skyscrapers and other modern developments.

Great shopping is also found in Tokyo. The wealthy go to Ginza. Glitzy stores and trendy boutiques carry the latest fashions. Tech lovers visit Akihabara for its electronic goods. Many people shop Harajuku for its youthful fashions. Harajuku is Tokyo's center of teen fashion culture and street style. Young people come from across the city to see and be seen.

The Asakusa district is known for shopping and its temples.

Tokyo Is Expensive, But Public Services Help

It can take a lot of money to live in Tokyo. Food, clothing, and housing are expensive. The city has among the highest costs of living in the world. Wealthy people are less affected than poorer Japanese.

Some of the richest people in Tokyo live in Minato ward. Households there make an average 11.1 million yen ($98,000) a year. Earnings are often lower in other areas. People to the east in Koto and to the south in Ota have incomes one-third that amount. On the city's border, some households earn less than one-quarter of Minato average incomes.

Tokyo has obvious gaps in wealth. But it ranks among the most livable cities in the world. This ranking includes safety, environment, health care, infrastructure, and education. Poorer people in Japan's capital benefit from public services that help improve their quality of life.

People can buy clothes, fish, dried food, spices, and many other things at local street markets.

Tokyo's schools try to provide children with a high-quality education. Students attend six years of elementary school. Three years of junior high follow. Another three years of study take place in high school. Many students go on to college.

Residents and visitors alike enjoy Tokyo's vibrant streets. People buy produce and other goods at local stalls. Restaurants serve foods for every taste. And the night brings people out to arcades and other fun spots.

No. 2
Where Tokyo ranks among the world's most expensive cities

- Only Hong Kong is costlier to live in.
- Living costs in Tokyo differ between neighborhoods.
- Wealthy people often live together in neighborhoods the poor cannot afford.

THINK ABOUT IT

Are there large gaps in wealth where you live? What can be done to help people who don't have enough money to buy what they need?

12

Residents Enjoy Many National Holidays

Awa Odori is the largest dance festival in Tokyo.

People in Tokyo celebrate many holidays. New Year is the most important. Cultural events occur over several days. Japanese pray at shrines and temples. Many gather for celebrations meant to bring good luck. Some shop deals at local stores.

Coming of Age Day takes place in January. People turning age 20 during a given year are celebrated. Tokyo residents also revere elders. Respect for the Aged Day occurs in September. People visit parents and grandparents. Many volunteer to help the elderly in their communities.

Other holidays celebrate historic events. National Foundation Day is the anniversary of modern Japan's birth. Constitution Memorial Day marks the date the current form of law was established. And Showa Day celebrates an emperor from the last century.

Festivals are another important part of life in Tokyo. Locals and tourists alike enjoy the Bunkyo Cherry Blossom

16
Number of national holidays in Japan

- The country is among world leaders in public holidays.
- People usually have the day off from work on these days.
- Officials hope holidays will help keep people from working too much.

CELEBRATING NATURE

Many Japanese worship nature. Several national holidays celebrate the outdoors. Spring Equinox Day in March is one. Greenery Day in May is another. People often spend time outdoors. Marine Day occurs in July. Japanese recognize how the Pacific Ocean benefits the nation. And Mountain Day is in August. Many people hike nearby areas on this holiday.

Festival. People walk among 120 cherry trees in spring bloom. A few weeks later is the Mount Takao Spring Festival.

About 3 million visitors enjoy nature and religious ceremonies. In summer, the Bunkyo Hydrangea Festival draws flower lovers.

Fun Facts about Tokyo

- Area of the Tokyo Metropolis: 846 square miles (2,191 sq km). Population: 13 million.

- Area of Greater Tokyo: 5,243 square miles (13,556 sq km). Population: 38 million.

- Vending machines are everywhere. Even at the top of Mount Fuji. They sell everything from hot coffee in cans to T-shirts and toys.

- Mt. Fuji can be seen from Tokyo, but not every day. It's only visible for about 80 days a year. At other times, it's covered by clouds.

- Tokyo's Tsukiji Market is the world's busiest seafood market. A tuna auction takes place at 5 a.m. Visitors can snag free tickets at 4 a.m.

- Tokyo Tower gets repainted every five years. This takes almost a year and 7,500 gallons of paint.

- So many people ride the Tokyo commuter trains that the city hires "pushers" for rush hours. They literally push people into the train, squeezing in as many as possible.

- The city has more than 6,000 parks and gardens. Together they cover more than 2,470 acres (1,000 hectares).

- Aragawa in Tokyo is one of the most expensive steak houses in the world. It has its own herd of cattle.

- Disney's first park outside the United States was Tokyo Disneyland. It opened in 1983. Nearly 18 million people visited in 2018.

Where in the World?

Tokyo

Glossary

archipelago
A group of islands.

boutique
A small shop selling goods.

contemporary
From the present time.

cuisine
A style of cooking.

gross domestic product (GDP)
Value of goods and services made within a country.

Michelin stars
An international rating system for restaurants.

modernization
The process of using technology to meet new needs.

population density
Average number of people living over a particular area.

prefecture
A district or county.

prosper
To do well or succeed in business.

revere
To show great respect.

terminal
A place where people and goods are transferred after travel.

transmit
To pass information from one place to another.

typhoon
A powerful storm in the Indian Ocean or western Pacific Ocean.

Read More

Claybourne, Anna. *Tokyo City Trails: Secrets, Stories, and Other Cool Stuff.* London, UK: Lonely Planet Publications, 2017.

Denson, Abby. *Cool Japan Guide: Fun in the Land of Manga, Lucky Cats, and Ramen.* Rutland, VT: Tuttle Publishing, 2014.

Story, Marie. *Traveling Through Tokyo: A Kids' Travel Guide.* San Antonio, TX: Paper Newt, 2017.

Visit 12StoryLibrary.com

Scan the code or use your school's login at **12StoryLibrary.com** for recent updates about this topic and a full digital version of this book. Enjoy free access to:

- Digital ebook
- Breaking news updates
- Live content feeds
- Videos, interactive maps, and graphics
- Additional web resources

Note to educators: Visit 12StoryLibrary.com/register to sign up for free premium website access. Enjoy live content plus a full digital version of every 12-Story Library book you own for every student at your school.

Index

About the Author

Douglas J. Fehlen is an elementary educator. He is also a longtime editor of books for kids and teens. Douglas lives in Minnesota with his wife, their two dutiful dogs, and one mischievous cat.